Imprint

Concept, Text and Layout:
Bernhard Helminger

Photos: Katrin Georg, Bernhard Helminger, Reinhard Tripp, Gerhard Vlcek

Editing: Sitta Kleinschmid

English Translation: Prof. Thomas Ball, Freilassing/Germany

ISBN: 978-3-902692-34-4
Fourth edition: May 2015

Publisher:
Colorama Verlagsgesellschaft mbH,
5020 Salzburg, Gabelsbergerstraße 25,
Tel. +43 (0)662 840899–0, Fax DW 44,
office@colorama.at, www.colorama.at

Print: "agensketterl" Druckerei GmbH, Mauerbach. Printed in Austria.

Bernhard Helminger thanks all who have contributed to the success of this illustrated guide: Susanne Leibrecht, Reinhard H. Gruber, Florian Monheim, Daniela Tollmann, Roman Szczepaniak, Dietmar Vettermann, Martin Czernin, Konstanze Kathan, Birgit Watzinger, Rainer Fankhauser, Berufsfeuerwehr der Stadt Wien, Paul K. A. Kunsky, Alfred Kriegler, Monika Frassine, Monika Scheinost, Maria Gattringer, Erich Peischl, Michael Unger, Olivia Harrer, Reinhard Tripp, Sabine Schally, Jörg Buß, Maria Wiesinger, Renate Scharringer, Irina Abajew, Theresia Pircher, Anja Reisch, Gertrude Salomon, Vivienne Kaier, Pater Matthias Schlögl, Manfred Zips, Bontus Immobilien.

Contents

St. Stephen's Cathedral (Stephansdom)

St. Stephen's Cathedral is Vienna's most recognizable landmark and Austria's finest Gothic edifice.

In 1147, a consecrated Romanesque church stood on the site of the present building, surrounded by a cemetery. The West Façade dates from the 13th century along with the two "Pagan" Towers and the Giant's Door/Riesentor.

Between 1304 and 1340, Dukes Albrecht I and Albrecht II erected the Gothic (Albertine) Choir; the South Tower (rising to just under 137m/449ft.) finally attained completion in 1433.

The smaller and uncompleted North Tower remains a mystery. About 1450 the architect Hans Puchsbaum was to have designed a tower exceeding the size and grandeur of the South Tower. Even today it is unclear as to whether work had to be suspended in 1515 due to financial reasons or whether by then the (Gothic) style was no longer in tune with the spirit of the times. The fact is that the tower reveals a height of only 68m/223 ft. It was not until 1578 that the Saphoy Brothers topped the Gothic torso with a conspicuous Renaissance cap.

Master sculptor Anton Pilgram was responsible for a number of interior features created between 1511 and 1516, as for example the cathedral pulpit and organ base. Nevertheless, following general conversion to the Baroque style in the 17th century, existing Gothic furnishings are fragmentary. None of the original 34 Gothic winged altars has been preserved. The Wiener Neustadt Altar of 1447 – one of the art-historical gems of the present-day interior furnishings – was only added to the Cathedral in 1883. While the Cathedral remained unscathed during World War II, civilian plunderers set the building on fire in April 1945 causing serious damage. The timber framework of the roof was devastated by the flames and the great 22-ton cathedral bell, the "Pummerin", came crashing down out of its wooden bell cage. Reconstruction work commenced after the end of the war. In 1952 the Cathedral was reopened with a festive inauguration of the recast bell.

Pictured above: The altarpiece of 1474 of the "Schottenkirche", founded by Iro-Scottish monks, depicts the cathedral largely as we know it today.

Soaring to a height of just under 137m/449ft., the **South Tower** of St. Stephen's Cathedral projects above Vienna's City Centre (above). The West Façade with the two Pagan Towers/**Heidentürme** dates back to the construction period extending from 1230 to 1245 (top right).

Unlike other comparable European cathedrals, St. Stephen's has no extended cathedral square. **Stephansplatz** is totally undersized and out of proportion to the huge cathedral church (bottom right).

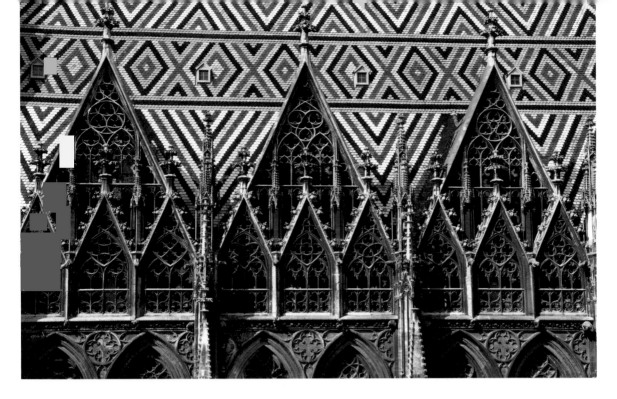

Wimpergs (top) – ornamental gable-like façade copings – are frequently encountered in Gothic architecture. They serve to reduce wind pressure on the roof with its some 230,000 tiles. **Pinnacles** serve to weight down the buttresses while stabilizing the structure downwards (bottom).

The **main or centre aisle** of the Cathedral (right). The **high altar** (top left) is an early Baroque masterpiece built to a design of the Pock Brothers. Another art-historical treasure piece is the Madonna of the Servants/**Dienstbotenmadonna.** This statue dates back to the time between 1280 and 1320 (bottom left).

Sculptural Gothic masterpieces in St. Stephen's Cathedral (pictured clockwise beginning top left): The **Wiener Neustadt Altar** of 1447; the impressive **Gothic vaulted ceiling** of the triple-nave Cathedral; at the base of the organ a **self-portrait of the sculptor Anton Pilgram,** who crafted essential interior furnishings between 1511 and 1516; detail at the base of the Pilgram pulpit showing a window-gawking **figure known as the Fenstergucker** (fenster = window; gucker = person who gawks); **the Pilgram pulpit** (page 12).

Out and About in Medieval Vienna

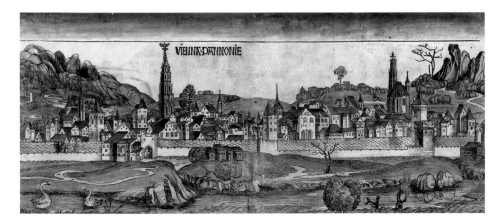

While ninth-century Vienna boasted a fortress, market ("Hoher Markt") and church (Ruprechtskirche), the city did not attain historical significance until after 1130 when the Babenberg dynasty acquired Merchants' Square. Vienna's rapid development was closely associated with Heinrich II (1107–1177), who in 1145 turned Vienna into the capital of what eventually became the Duchy of Ostarrichi (Austria). Heinrich erected a palace and domestic outbuilding on a site still known as "Am Hof" (royal court). In 1147 a small church was consecrated, then outside the town walls – the forerunner of today's St. Stephen's Cathedral. Heinrich II also founded the Iro-Scottish Monastery/Schottenkloster in which he lies buried.

Alighting at the Metro Station "Stubentor" one encounters remains of the city wall erected by Duke Leopold V (1157–1194) and demolished in the 19th century. The two main gates leading into the city were the Carinthia Gate/Kärntnertor in the south and the Red Tower Gate/Rotenturmtor in the north. Initial mention of "Kärntnerstraße" goes back to 1257. This road eventually became known as "Venedigerstraße" owing to its further course continuing on right through to Venice.

Adriatic trading proceeded from "Neuer Market". The size of two football fields, this trading place provided adequate space for numerous buyers and sellers in addition to artisans.

In line with the rapid growth of the city, the Schottenkloster was soon joined by other monasteries, the Franciscan Friars being the first, followed by Dominican and Augustinian orders. By1500, some 750 monks were responsible for the pastoral care of Vienna's 20,000 inhabitants. As far back as 1237 mention is made of a school close to St. Stephen's. Opposite the cathedral church, a field dispensary "Zum goldenen Greif" was founded in 1320. This still operates today under the name "Alte Feldapotheke" (Old Field Dispensary).

Fires posed a serious threat, frequently devastating up to one third of the city. Erection of the city walls coincided with structural improvements involving the use of stone and tiled roofs, eventually followed by chimneys, fire walls and merlons.

There is mention of a hangman in the 13th century who later took up quarters in Rauhensteingasse Lane. This hangman's house ("Schergenhaus") also served as a jail and torture chamber.

Winding roadways were common in medieval times and served to impede enemy assault. About 1500, Emperor Ferdinand I introduced a type of tennis game to Vienna from Spain resulting in a number of ballgame houses or halls being erected. Certain street names are still a reminder of this.

Pictured above: Historic view of Vienna taken in 1493 from Hartmann Schedel's World Chronicle. Left: Griechengasse.

Kärntner Straße (pictured on page 16) already existed at the time of the Romans. In medieval times it linked the town centre with Carinthia Gate/Kärntnertor. Today it is a shopping boulevard similar to those normally found in larger European cities. The oldest building still existent in Kärntner Straße is **Palais Ester-hàzy** which now houses a gambling casino (top left).

Located a stone's throw away is Neuer Markt with the **Capuchin Church** (above right). The **Imperial Crypt** contains the remains of all German and Austrian emperors since 1633 except for one. The larger image above shows the tombs of Empress Elisabeth known as "Sisi" (1837–1898) (sarcophagus on left), Emperor Franz Joseph I (1830–1916, centre) and Crown Prince Rudolph (1858–1889, right).

Graben (top) is another of Vienna's popular shopping malls. **Kohlmarkt** (below) is commonly known as Luxury Mile on account of the close network of jewellers and top-class brands found there. The street name has been in existence since the 14th century, the time when charcoal was sold on this spot. In the background we catch a glimpse of St. Michael's Gate leading to the Hofburg Imperial Palace (see page 26 onwards).

A few feet away from "Graben" there stood a medieval church. This was demolished in 1661 following a fire. The famous architect Lucas von Hildebrandt was responsible for a new baroque church built on this site – **St. Peter's** *– work on which commenced in 1703 (above).*

The Viennese Coffeehouse Tradition

Vienna's first café was founded by Georg Kolschitzky who received some sacks of Turkish coffee beans as a gift for supplying intelligence to the Imperial Army that led to its overcoming the Turkish siege of 1683. In defiance of changing fashions, the Viennese coffee house developed and retained its typical form gradually over the centuries. Distinctive features, apart from a buffet and newspaper table, include large wall-mirrors and marble tables with matching plush couches and chairs. A Viennese café is an oasis of peace and quiet where coffee drinking is something of a ceremony. Guests can read newspapers undisturbed for hours on end and sample coffee in up to 24 different varieties. Vienna boasts roughly 1,000 coffee houses, the smallest ("Kleines Café") on Franziskanerplatz, the largest in Ringstraße.

*A legendary establishment is the coffeehouse set up by **Leopold Hawelka** born in 1911 (passed away 2011, top). Other cafés pictured are **Café Sperl** located in Vienna's 6ᵗʰ District (central photo), **Café Prückel,** Ringstraße (bottom right) and **Café Central** in Herrengasse (bottom left).*

With its magnificent city palais, **Freyung Square** (above) is one of the finest in Vienna's Old Town. The Iro-Scottish Monastery founded in 1155 has continued to dominate the square down to the present day. Freyung Square is chiefly known for its markets, in particular the **Easter Market** (bottom right) or the Old Vienna Christmas Fair. In Ferstel Palais a splendid marble-lined passage-way **(Freyung Passage)** forms a link to Herrengasse (bottom left).

"Am Hof" Square (top) lays claim to historic significance: it was here – in the heart of medieval Vienna – that the Babenbergs resided (predecessors of the Habsburgs) from 1155 up to about 1280. The church is essentially Gothic but was given an impressive baroque façade in 1607 following an outbreak of fire. Bottom: **Judenplatz,** centre of the Vienna's Jewish community during the Middle Ages.

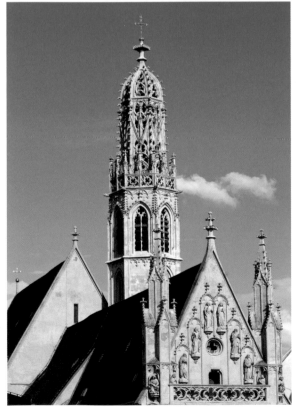

The **Ankeruhr Clock** on Hohen Markt Square. This horologic masterpiece designed in art nouveau style was erected in 1914 (see larger view at top). The Bohemian Court Chancellery/**Böhmische Hofkanzlei** built from 1709 to 1714 by Fischer von Erlach (above) now houses the Constitutional Court. **Maria am Gestade** (left) is one of Vienna's oldest churches; the characteristic Gothic spire underwent completion in 1428.

First recorded in 1200, **Ruprechtskirche** (above) is Vienna's oldest surviving church. It is dedicated to St. Rupert, the patron saint of salt merchants and founder of the City of Salzburg.

The baroque **Dominican Church** (top right) took more than 40 years to build, finally undergoing completion in 1674. This is the second largest church in Vienna. The **Jesuit Church** (bottom right), an early baroque edifice, owes its present-day appearance to the architect Andrea Pozzo.

The **Mozarthaus Vienna** museum on Domgasse no. 5 (pictured above) serves as a reminder that Wolfgang Amadeus Mozart lived here between 1784 and 1787. During his stay Mozart composed the opera "The Marriage of Figaro". This is the only one of Mozart's apartments in Vienna that still exists today. The narrow lanes built around Ruprechtskirche are known as the Bermuda Triangle/**Bermudadreieck** (picture below).

Imperial Vienna – Hofburg Court Palace

Although no exact date is traceable, the Bohemian King Ottokar II Premysl, began building a fortress and moat in the mid 13th century or thereabouts exactly on the site where today the Swiss Wing of the Hofburg is located. By the time this edifice received first official mention in 1279 (then not a palace but merely a fortification complex with a keep) Ottokar had already been defeated. He was followed by the first Roman-German king from the House of Habsburg, Rudolf I.

The Hofburg is anything but a uniform structure. In fact it developed over a period of six centuries. Extensions continued on this irregular set of buildings from the time of Ferdinand I, who reigned from 1531 to 1564 and who was the first of the Habsburgs to feel at home in Vienna, through to Franz Joseph I (1848–1916, *top)* who set the course for Vienna becoming a metropolis. Development took place without respect for architectural perspective. Accordingly, the huge complex resembles an incidental hotchpotch of widely differing styles.

Maria Theresia and her husband, Franz Stephan I. of Lorraine (1740–1765) took up their winter residence in the suite of the Leopold Wing situated towards the inner courtyard and named after her

grandfather Leopold I (1657–1705) who had commissioned this resplendent part of the Hofburg to be built. Their son, Josef II (1780–1790), occupied the rooms situated adjacent with a view overlooking the moats and bastions of the town fortifications (now Heldenplatz Square). Josef's brother and heir to the throne, Leopold II (1790–1792), spent his brief two-year reign in the Amalie Wing, the northwest termination of the inner courtyard built in the 15th century and rebuilt by Rudolf II (1576–1612). Exactly opposite, in the Swiss Wing, Franz II/I (1792–1835) – first Emperor of Austria from 1804 to 1806 and last Emperor of the Holy Roman Empire – took up what were very much civil quarters. His son, Ferdinand (1835–1848) preferred the Leopold Wing.

His nephew and successor Franz Joseph I chose to reside in the majestic northeast wing of the palace built by Karl VI (1711-1740) which underwent completion as an "Imperial Chancellery" towards the close of the 19th century. Karl I (1916–1918), the last Austrian emperor, finally held office in the Amalie Wing. The inner courtyard, also called "Franzensplatz", is thus surrounded by imperial residential quarters.

Neue Hofburg (pictured above) is the most recent edifice in the imperial residential quarters and represents the style known as Historicism that developed along Ringstraße as from 1860. The equestrian statues in front of Neue Hofburg are monuments dedicated to the two commanders Archduke Karl and Prince Eugène.

The Outer Castle Gate/**Äußere Burgtor** (pictured on page 29, bottom left) was erected from 1821 to 1824, Napoleon's troops having destroyed the old gate.

Joseph Emanuel Fischer von Erlach had already planned **St. Michael's Wing back** in 1726. Nevertheless, it took well over 150 years to complete this impressive edifice with its awe-inspiring dome after the old Imperial Court Theatre/Burgtheater had been removed to Ringstraße (pictured on page 29, bottom right).

The Lippizzan/**Lipizzaner** (page 30) is the world's oldest breed of horse, its principal breeding place being the **Spanish Riding School** founded in 1565. Originally an institution for training the imperial family in horsemanship, it now ranks as a UNESCO World Heritage Site. Demonstrations in the **Winter Riding School** inaugurated in 1735 (larger image above and on left) are just as much a visitor attraction as guided tours of the Imperial Stables/**Stallburg** vis-à-vis (above).

The red-black Swiss Gate/**Schweizertor** (top) on which the titles of Emperor Ferdinand I are displayed along with the insignia of the Order of the Golden Fleece forms the entrance to the Swiss Court (Schweizer Hof). This corresponds in its form to the 13th century castle except that it was converted to the Renaissance style during the mid 16th century. The Swiss Court contains the Gothic Court Chapel rebuilt in the 15th century and the Imperial Treasury/Schatzkammer. Viewed on right, top to bottom: **Austrian imperial crown; cradle of Napoleon's son,** a gift of the City of Paris to Napoleon Bonaparte and Marie Louise; **emerald unguentarium** of 1641, one of the world's largest emeralds.

*The Royal Library (today the **Austrian National Library**) was designed according to the plans of Johann Bernhard Fischer von Erlach and underwent completion in 1735. The Baroque Great Hall (pictured above) ranks among the world's most impressive library rooms.*

The Amalie Residence/**Amalienburg** (top) is one of the oldest buildings of Hofburg Court Palace and was erected as a residence for Emperor Rudolf II (1552–1612). Originally this edifice stood alone but now forms a link to the Leopold Wing (view on left) and Imperial Chancellery Wing (right).
Bottom: **Josefsplatz Square.** Left: entrance to the National Library; right: Redouten Wing.

The **Albertina** in the Archduke Albrecht Palais hou-ses a distinguished graphic-art collection with ex-hibits ranging from the Late Gothic period through to contemporary art (larger image, top). Many of the Habsburgs exchanged their marriage vows in the **Augustinian Church** consecrated in 1349 (left). Above: **Palm House in Castle Gardens.**

The "Ring" – Vienna's Prestigious Boulevard

A wall surrounding the heart of Vienna's inner city had already existed in medieval times. After the First Turkish Siege in 1529 this defence construction underwent substantial reinforcement. To provide an unobstructed view of potential assailants, a glacis – 300-400m (984-1312ft.) wide strip of meadowland – was laid out ahead of the bastions. By the mid 19th century at the latest, the city wall had ceased to have any further military significance and the fortifications were found to be hampering what were rapidly progressing urban development plans. While the citizens of Vienna had meanwhile come to appreciate the park-like glacis with its refreshment pavilions for its recreational facilities, Emperor Franz Joseph I made a bold decision on December 20, 1857 for the city wall to be razed to the ground and a boulevard to be erected in its place.

85 projects, each containing a ground plan for the "Ring", had been submitted by summer 1858. However, it was to take 16 years for the fortifications to disappear altogether. The new and stately causeway was financed from urban extension funds. Only the City Hall/Rathaus was erected by the City of Vienna. Generously laid out recreational spaces were created, e.g. City Park, Castle Gardens, Public Gardens or Rathaus Park.

For the architectural design of the buildings erected between 1860 and 1890, older styles were mainly resorted to e.g. Gothic, Renaissance or Baroque. Today, this style of architecture has come to be known as "Historicism" or in this case (peculiar to Vienna) "Ringstraße Style".

The "Ring" is more or less circular in shape and is well over 5 km (3 miles) in length, subdivided into nine sections from "Stubenring" to "Schottenring". Only Franz-Josefs-Kai situated north-east deviates from the strict geometrical pattern of the route.

The "Ring", which had been constructed for prestige purposes, was to be provided with an additional transport route running parallel. Nowadays this is identified by a variety of different street names, the Viennese themselves referring to it as "No. 2 Line" alluding to the former tramway lines E2, G2 and H2 replaced in 1980 by Metro Line U2.

Treated in this chapter are all buildings located along the "Ring" or "No. 2 Line", regardless of whether these are classical "Ringstraße" structures or – in the case of St. Charles's Church/Karlskirche for example – had existed earlier. The following photographic tour begins at the Urania and ends at Schottenring.

Urania (top) located at the point where the Vienna River meets up with the Danube Canal, was built in 1909 according to the plans of art nouveau architect Max Fabiani, a student of Otto Wagner. The first museum to be built in the "Ring" was designed by Heinrich von Ferstel, its present day funktion is that of a Museum of Applied Art, better known as **MAK** (pictures below: Neo-Renaissance façade, Columned Hall).

One of the most frequently photographed monuments of Vienna is the **gilt bronze statue of Johann Strauss II** (top) erected in the Vienna City Park/Stadtpark. Designed by Edmund Hellmer, it was unveiled on June 26, 1921.

To provide recreational facilities for the Viennese citizens, the City of Vienna built a spa centre/**Kursalon** from 1865 to 1867 (left). Today this has become an established venue for balls, weddings and other events.

St. Charles's Church/**Karlskirche** ranks among the most illustrious baroque places of worship north of the Alps (see page 40 and above). It owes its Italian character to Johann Bernhard Fischer von Erlach, a star architect of the period, who had undergone training in Rome. The façade symbolizes a Roman temple portico; the adjacent columns are modelled on Trajan's Column in Rome; the spiral staircases have their origins in the Eternal City. Bottom: **View of the High Altar.**

The Vienna Secession

In 1897 a group of fine artists formed around the painter Gustav Klimt seceded from the conservative-minded Artists' Union and founded the Vienna Secession Association. The related genre is still known even today as the Viennese Art Nouveau Style.

Located not far from St. Charles's Church is the **Secession Exhibition House** *(top right) and the* **Karlsplatz Metropolitan Railway Station** *(bottom right). Pictures to the left: The* **Church am Steinhof** *constructed by Otto Wagner in Vienna's 14th District.*

Located along "No. 2 Line", originally a transport route running parallel to the "Ring", is a building of special importance to art lovers of the arts: The Golden Hall/**Goldenen Saal** (left) of the Viennese Music Association/**Wiener Musikvereins** (top) inaugurated in 1870 is where the annual New Year's Concerts of the Vienna Philharmonic Orchestra take place.

When in 1857 it was resolved to construct a stately boulevard, the first monumental structure planned to be built was the Imperial Court Opera House – now the **Vienna State Opera.** Neo-Renaissance in style, the edifice was designed by the Viennese architects Sicard von Sicardsburg and Van der Nüll and inaugurated on May 25, 1869 with a first-night performance of Mozart's "Don Giovanni". Pictured above: the **grand staircase** and **auditorium** accommodating audiences of over 2,000.
Pages 44/45: The **State Opera viewed from the "Ring".**

The Vienna Opera Ball/**Wiener Opernball** is Austria's leading high-society event. Its roots go back to the year 1877 when a soirée was first held there. Today, some 12,000 amusement-seekers culled from a variety of cultural, industrial and political spheres pour into the State Opera, whose lustrous ballroom has to be prepared within a short space of 70 hours.

The two buildings housing the **Museum of Fine Arts** and the **Museum of Natural History** (aerial view, pages 50/51) are absolutely symmetrical and formed part of the unfinished "Imperial Forum" an architectural project devised by Gottfried Semper originally intended to form the climax to the "Ring". The memorial between the twin museums shows Empress Maria Theresia. The Museum of Fine Arts evolved from Habsburg collections and ranks among the principal museums of this kind worldwide.

Illustrations on this pages:
Façade of the Museum of Fine Arts (Kunsthistorisches Museum, pictured above),
staircase and **vestibule**.

Prominent exhibits from the Museum of Fine Arts: **"Large Self-portrait"** *(right) by Rembrandt (1606–1669) and (far right)* **"The Fur"** *by Pieter Paul Rubens (1577–1640).*

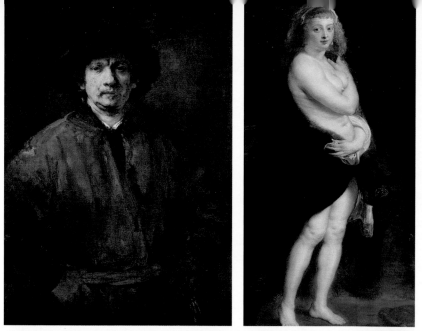

*The Museum Quarter/***Museumsquartier,** *opened in 2001, has proved a brilliant success. The former Imperial Stables (erected in 1725 by Fischer von Erlach) are devoted to contemporary art. On display in the Leopold Museum is the Leopold Collection (Schiele/Klimt), while the Museum of Modern Art, known simply as MUMOK, contains works representing Classic Modern Art including Warhol and Picasso.*

The **Austrian Houses of Parliament** (larger image above) is where the legislative body of the Republic, the National Council, convenes along with the Federal Council and the lesser important Provincial Chamber The building was designed by Theophil von Hansen in the Greco-Roman style and inaugurated in December 1883. Towering above the fountain is a 4m/13ft. high statue of Pallas Athene.

Situated almost opposite is the **Vienna Palace of Justice** (central pictures) constructed from 1875 to 1881 by Alexander Wielemans von Monteforte in the Neo-Renaissance style.

The Viennese Imperial Court Theatre/**Wiener Burgtheater** (right) is classed among the leading German-language theatres in Europe. Up to 1888 it was located on St. Michael's Square/ Michaelerplatz close to Hofburg Palace before removal to the Neo-Baroque edifice along the "Ring". The building was gutted after being hit by a bomb in 1945 and was not re-opened until ten years later. Design of the ceiling frescoes enhancing the two staircases included work by Gustav Klimt. Pictured above is the **Imperial Staircase.**

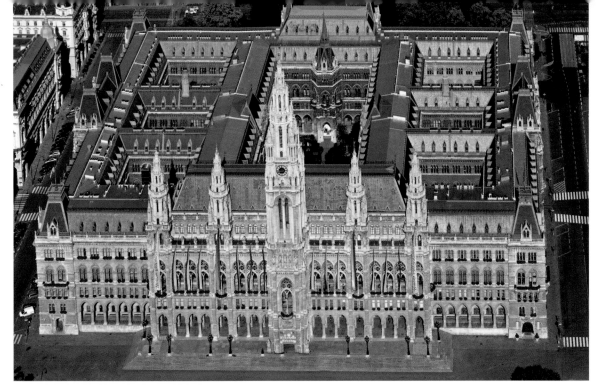

Vienna underwent substantial growth in 1850 when several suburbs were incorporated in the boundaries of the City. Accordingly, it was decided to build a larger City Hall/**Rathaus** along the "Ring". The façade is an outstanding example of Neo-Gothic civil architecture. The building measures 152m/498.7ft. in length and 127m/416.7ft. in width, and contains 1,575 rooms.

Once destined for political rallies, the square outside the City Hall **(Rathausplatz)** is nowadays used for all types of events, e.g. **Christmas markets** (top), **ice-skating** (right), cinema performances, classical concerts, etc. The **Life Ball,** Europe's largest charity event founded in 1992 for the benefit of persons infected with the HI virus and those suffering with AIDS, is an ear-splitting and colourful experience (above).

The **main building of the University** (top left) was erected between 1877 and 1884 by Heinrich von Ferstel who also designed the **Votive Church** (centre left), a token of humble gratitude paid by Emperor Franz Joseph I after surviving a (thwarted) assassination. The Neo-Gothic towers rise to a height of 99m/324.5ft. Top right: the **Stock Exchange**. After suffering serious damage in World War II, inauguration of the 73m/ 239.5ft. high-rise **Ring Tower** (centre right) in 1955 proved a milestone in the reconstruction of the City.

Baroque Palaces – Schönbrunn and Belvedere

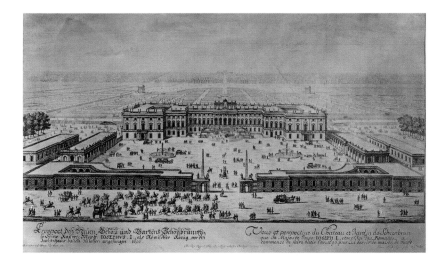

Among the most popular sights of Vienna are the two imperial baroque palaces and residences of the Habsburgs, Schönbrunn and Belvedere. While Belvedere is situated in direct proximity of the "Ring", Schönbrunn is located about 5 km/3 miles away from the city centre in Vienna's 13th District.

Vienna owes its important monuments, such as Karlskirche or the Great Hall of the National Library, to the celebrated Baroque architect Johann Bernhard Fischer von Erlach (1656–1723). Schönbrunn Palace is also based on his plans even if Maria Theresia, who loved the place, set about having it converted to a residential palace designed by Nikolaus Pacassi as from 1744.

The historical significance of Schönbrunn is immense: for centuries it was the summer residence of the Habsburgs. Napoleon took up quarters here between 1806 and 1809 as well as the European rulers during the Vienna Congress of 1814/15. Emperor Franz Joseph I was born and died in Schönbrunn. In 1918, Emperor Karl I signed the document renouncing all participation in state affairs, thus sealing the end of the Danube Monarchy.

Following expropriation of the Imperial Court, ownership of the palace passed to the Republic of Austria. It became recognized by UNESCO as a world heritage site in 1996 and attracts approximately two million visitors a year.

After final victory over the Turks in 1683 and the annexation of Hungary, Vienna entered a glorious era. A spectacular witness of this period is the summer residence of the great military leader Prince Eugène of Savoy – Belvedere Palace. The baroque complex comprises the stately palace "Upper Belvedere" constructed from 1721 to 1723. The conspicuously smaller garden palace "Lower Belvedere" had already undergone completion in 1716. The two are linked by attractive gardens.

Both these palaces were designed by Johann Lucas von Hildebrandt (1668–1745), whose fame as an architect is comparable to that of Johann Bernhard Fischer von Erlach. After Prince Eugène's death, Belvedere came under the ownership of the Habsburgs. Today it houses an art collection of significance – the Belvedere Austrian Gallery.

Erected in 1775, the **Gloriette** (top) provides a spectacular view of the gardens covering 1.6 sq.m/17.2 sq.ft. In 1880 Emperor Franz Joseph I commissioned the **Palm House** (bottom) to be built in order to create a worthy setting for the Habsburg collection of tropical plants.

The photo on pages 62/63 shows **Schönbrunn Palace,** north façade with forecourt.

Top: View of the gardens from the Gloriette and the **south façade of Schönbrunn Palace.**

Emperor Franz (I) Stephan of Lorraine, who left it to his wife Maria Theresia to manage the state affairs, devoted himself to natural sciences. In 1752 he founded **Schönbrunn Zoological Park** *(central photos) and one year later the Botanical Gardens. The zoo is the oldest in the world. It catered for a sensation in 2007 with the birth of panda baby Fu Long. Successful breeding of polar bears, elephants and Siberian tigers also takes place here.*

Approximately 40m/130ft. in length, the **Grand Gallery** (top left) forms the heart of the palace and is now used for festive events. The ceiling frescoes are the work of the Italian artist Gregorio Guglielmi. Other state apartments: **Rösselzimmer,** literally Stallions Room (top right); **Marie Antoinette Salon** (centre left); **Chinese Salon** (centre right) used by Maria Theresia for privy conferences; **Vieux Laque Salon** (bottom right) Emperor Franz (I) Stephan's study.

In 1736 the Habsburg-Lorraine dynasty was formed as a result of the marriage of the Duke of Lorraine, later to become Emperor Franz (I) Stephan of Lorraine, with Archduchess and Habsburg heiress **Maria Theresia** *(pictured above).*

It was a happy marriage from which 16 children proceeded. Though never crowned empress, Maria Theresia managed the affairs of the monarchy for 40 years. She implemented essential reforms and set numerous monuments in memory of herself.

From the very outset, **Upper Belvedere** (right) was planned for prestige purposes, the lower palace mainly being used as a residence. The **Main Gate** (top) supports the armorial bearings of Prince Eugène, the lion. The **Sala Terrena** on the ground floor (above) is an Italian-style garden hall, whose design may be ascribed to the years of study in Rome by the architect, Johann Lukas von Hildebrandt.

Lower Belvedere *(top) had already undergone completion in 1716. Essential structures include the Oran-*
*gery and Imperial Stables/Prunkstall. The **Marble Hall** (centre left) contains the original of the Donner*
*Fountain, a lead casting sculpted by Georg Raphael Donner. In the **Golden Room** stands a marble statue*
of Prince Eugène crafted about 1718 by Balthasar Permoser (centre right).

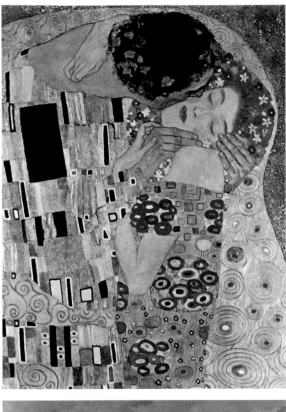

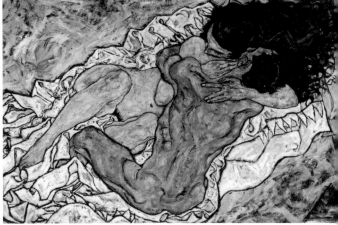

The **art collection at Belvedere** is one of the best known in the world, mainly due to the proud display of works by Gustav Klimt. Pictured top left: **"The Kiss"**. Other famous works include Claude Monet's **"Path in Monet's Garden at Giverny"** (top right); self-portrait Ferdinand Georg Waldmüller (left) and **"The Embrace"** by Egon Schiele (centre right).

Modern Vienna, a place worth living in

If a study conducted by the Mercer Consulting Agency comparing 221 metropolises is anything to go by, Vienna ranks as the world's most congenial city. Vienna outscores all others on account of its optimum infrastructure and ranks globally as one of the safest capitals. The probability of falling victim to murder in Vienna is six times less than say in New York. Environmental protection is likewise exemplary. Scarcely any other city is able to lay claim to so much verdancy: dozens of parks are an attraction in the city centre, notable recreation areas include the Vienna Woods along with beauty spots situated on the banks of the Danube e.g. Lobau National Park, the Prater Water Meadows or Danube Island.

Vienna offers a sensational variety of musical and theatrical events apart from being Europe's leading exhibition and trade-fair base. Those in search of youth cultural events may need to look closer but these do exist: innovative galleries and art centres such as "inoperable", "das weisse Haus", "Magazin", "Metalab" or "eSeL Rezeption" as well as music festivals, for example "BLK River" or "sound:frame" cater for something new and fresh. Youth and student rendezvous in Vienna are to be found in the areas surrounding "Naschmarkt", "Karmelitermarkt" and "Yppenplatz" as well as in the Museum Quarter and in parts of Districts 6 to 8, i.e. Mariahilf, Neubau and Josefstadt. In addition there are off-theatres (Rabenhof, Schauspielhaus), an active cinematic scene (Oscar Academy Award for Stefan Ruzowitzky's "The Counterfeiters" in 2008), designer shops (especially in Lindengasse) and design and fashion events (Vienna Fashion Week, Vienna Design Week, trade fairs "Modepalast/Fashion Palace", "Home Depot", "Blickfang"). The weekly newspaper "Falter" provides an overview of Vienna's variegated cultural and music scene.

Most illustrated guides of this kind are usually limited to portraying historic monuments of the Gothic, Renaissance or Baroque eras. Applied to Vienna, this may sound like an understatement. After all, a specific art movement was coined well over a century ago: the Viennese Art Nouveau or Secessionist Style. Also as regards contemporary architecture, Vienna is an exciting place to explore: With the establishment of UNO City, official seat of the United Nations, an ambitious construction project was launched in the 1970s emerging in a new suburb on the left bank of the Danube close to Empire Bridge/Reichsbrücke.

In February 2014, the first of two DC-Towers was completed. The skyscraper designed by French architect Dominique Perrault reaches a height of 220 meters (720 ft).

Naschmarkt *is a Viennese speciality. The hustle and bustle characterizing this market contributes a great deal to the city's joie de vivre. About 1780 the market was moved to this spot from Freyung Square; its present-day form with typical stalls evolved during World War I. Trading takes place from Monday to Saturday, chiefly in fruit, vegetables, pastries, fish and meat. Between 2000 and 2004 many businesses were converted to restaurants.*

In 1972 heavy criticism was hurled at plans to land-fill **Danube Island/Donauinsel** (pictured above, viewed from Leopoldsberg) as part of an extensive project designed to counteract flooding. Today the Island, 21km/13 miles long and up to roughly 250m/820ft. broad, fulfils its purpose ideally and is regarded as indispensable by Viennese citizens as a recreational area. To landscape Danube Island, some 420 acres of woodland were planted.

The artificially created island divides the Danube up into two sections. While the **main (western) course** (right) is reserved for navigation, the New Danube waterway is open to bathers.

Hundertwasser-Krawina-Haus: Entwurf: Prof. J.Krawina; Maler: F. Hundertwasser; Planung: Prof. J.Krawina, P. Pelikan.

Contemporary architecture in Vienna: *The artist Friedensreich Hundertwasser (1928–2000) designed a residential house in the 3rd district of Vienna (**Hundertwasser-Krawina-Haus,** completed in 1985, pictured above) as well as the tower and façade of **Spittelau Refuse Incineration Plant** (1987, to the left).*

*On page 76: **Donaucity** with headquarters of the United Nations (large photo), the **Millennium Tower** (bottom left) and the **Vienna Twin Towers** (bottom right).*

The Wiener Prater

In most cases, the Wiener Prater is associated solely with the world-famous amusement park. It is frequently overlooked that this is a spacious public park, large parts of which still consist of river meadowland. The area of the Prater extends to 6 sq.km/2.3 square miles, three times larger than the Principality of Monaco. In 1564 Emperor Maximillian succeeded in purchasing the Prater from several landowners to create hunting grounds which he fenced off (hunting took place in the Prater up to 1920).

*The **Ernst Happel Stadium** (right) – named after the Viennese football legend – was erected in 1931. It boasts a capacity of some 50,000 spectators and ranks among Europe's most prestigious football arenas.*
*In 1766, Emperor Joseph II released the Prater for public use and in so doing laid the foundation stone for launching the **amusement park Wurstelprater** as it eventually became known as (bottom).*

*The Giant Wheel/**Riesenrad** (top) was inaugurated in 1897 to mark the golden jubilee of Emperor Franz Joseph I's accession to the throne. At that time it was the largest giant wheel in the world.*

Art and Photo Credits

All photos © Katrin Georg, Bernhard Helminger, Reinhard Tripp and Kurt Pultar with following exceptions: